D1432065

RAKING
LIGHT

Eric Langley

CARCANET

First published in Great Britain in 2017 by
Carcanet Press Ltd
Alliance House, 30 Cross Street
Manchester M2 7AQ
www.carcanet.co.uk

A CIP catalogue record for this book is available
from the British Library, ISBN 9781784103323

Typeset by Richard Skelton.
Printed & bound in England by SRP Ltd.
The publisher acknowledges financial assistance
from Arts Council England.

Contents

Raking Light

Glanced

I.

You lovely looker on and by and by and.
One-eyed Cupid, locked, cocks, and shot

Zeno's arrow at Zeuxis' grapes.
Shaft straight. The pointed

parabola arced its homeward hoops on its
wondering way through loop and loop

towards my eye's apple; its
projectory now arches down to heel to hit

or miss, may kiss the head or glance off
on bow bend or twisted thread.

My flighted hope: that bird cracks glass, and tumblers
beakers break on painted grapes

on picture plane or bounce back
deflected, as mote on float

reflected. Map the rebound 'cause
I am sore astound and all amazed,

while flecks dart and seeds quiver
quiver while the heavy freighted interim

divides
by half by half by half.

Split hairs or ends or seconds now sub-divide
by half and half, as hare's breath

on tortoise's collar falls and arrow
tip elbows each atom aside

to side or sneaks contracted
kiss, a peak, a contact passing

charge in the charge in the change
from Z to thee kinetic.

II.

Keep lovely looking on and over
looking keep looking till

your lead tip punctures what, back then, was
walnut, poppy, hemp, pine and olive; then

a resinous gloss, of Paris Green,
of arsenic, of mercuric sulphide;

then, later, *oglio cotto*, honeyed
lead oxide; then beeswax;

now, bladder-pod, ironweed, calendula,
sandmat, in slow drying strata

of alpha-linolenic, brittle as it brakes,
of crisp linoleic, of still wet oleic acid, still wet.

Then warp canvas warped.
Then wall.

III.

So keep on lovely looking on,
no overlook, from then to now, as now

the paste-board splits
and peck hits home and

dry eye and true to touch
and each grape breaks and

tortoise tumbles down hap with hare
and tip touches now, and now, and when

and then just so, soothed through
freeze frame and bending glass,

each hot pigment shot and then
and then, keep lovely looking till.

So glancing blown by,
so palpably hit away, so

keep so lovely looking still
keep lovely looking till

until each hungry bird
has flown and had his fill.

Albada: Pigeons on pink

I.

Don José, at dawn – at pinked half-light,
lit by blooms of orpiment lowlight,

hit in a masticot morning – stands
in reddish strands of saffron shade,

all tinged to the touch-up among this
ante meridiem pigment play, this play

of *Oker de Luce,* of cochineal, of all
of all those softish greenish vegetals,

of yellowed mineral bloom – a vegetable
lake of alum, salt and ashy alkali – and

all-for-all of the sharp smack tang of
spiced metallic oxide, of acumen and acid:

first, he dimly thinks, *I'll lay on soft,*
my whitest lead; then, he thinks, *I'll cut in cute*

with lac of carmine red; de Luce, he thinks,
for all her loose hair, more light and bright,

golden in the shadow of her chin, he thinks,
the rucks of her creamy white blouse;

and full inch-thick, full de Rouse, he thinks,
for her lips

II.

Don José, woken, winking, blinked-out, out
in the sunsight air of pinke-yellow,

dazed in quite the electric scatter, quite
the warmish Rayleigh, quite the Mei,

really pinked in the Galician umber air, just
a crumpled hardish thing, just past prime.

See, how the blend-line, the blur-line of
his thin nightcoat scumbles off in the ozone;

how it offs opaque in the envious streaks
of civil twilight, as the dawn's drive hints

in demi-tints, saddens his grosser edges –
her tits are rosy in the dawn, he dimly thinks –

how, it dissolves his quiet breath in
tender air, his body, his not yet solid extension:

and yet, he's not quite empty either, as that
would be pure space

III.

And with half of half his hottish mind still
up in bed, still on María, on Jill's mouth, and

still on rock doves, croodling, croodling,
the sluggish *el palomero* half or hardly hears

the *pink-pink* of fluttering spink or twink,
of a short sharp finch, its courting call,

its fine green shout-out to a lost flock,
from out there on the green beans, out beyond

the sill, from the senna bush, calling, calling;
or the grunt, the coo, and fall of

a choir-school booby, who's lost his mate; or
a proud wood pigeon, sat on the indigo gate.

Stopped on empty, in a moment's space
he hardly hears the liquid notes – *jug jug* –

the fast, the thick, the full-throated glottals
– *god! o god!* – that shoot the plum-tree leaves,

that lace the wriggling whitethorn, that seed
small explosions, rattles in the pomegranate tree

– *arise*, he thinks, *my love, my dove, my fair, and come
away*, he thinks, *in times of singing*

– and hardly then he hardly hears – *away,
away* – ignition-spark among our apples' pips:

it is – *our lips again* – a father's tale
distracts him

IV.

Instead, he almost hears in the *pink-pink*
– or *piz piz* perhaps – a longer longer echo

of his child's first words, when he called for
lapiz, López, pencil-leads, and the father, flinches.

Don José Ruiz y Blasco, the 'pigeon fancier,'
painter of *pipion,* new master at the *Bellas Artes,*

comes down across an orange flared kitchen,
to find Pablo, his Pablito, hard to his work:

look how he's lost in the arsenic sulfide glare,
he thinks, *in orpiment, lost; lost in masticot,*

lost to the saffron, to the English Pink, he thinks.
Look how my raw Jack kids and plucks

his nib, sees and sets and robs and steals
each squab – in more bright and brighter light –

and glibly gets and gets all these real these
really real pigeons

V.

The shock that shook that
hit me then: the hammered in-homing.

My guileless goblin pink, you have
mummed me quite, exposed my cheat,

revealed a likely scam: five pigeons
not quite tight to an ochre ground.

Your fledgling barbels, scrawled and
drawled across my careful crappers,

your unfledged gall-free jacobines
just so jogged and jotted off, in freefall,

have jostled off my cheaply cautious
chirpers, jumped my just-so crafted pickers,

and are the thing *per se*, perhaps;
and I'm bastard back, blackjacked.

I know I've nothing on this crafty kidder;
plucked quite naked, my care mere clay,

so: *here, come have them then, all these,*
my best brushes, my palette, gesso and linseed.

How hard things are as he strokes them,
his thumbs up across their throbbing vanes,

having his feel for the yellow fur, the
white flesh, the spiky wings and big head,

ruffling down the rachis, soft to the full to
the filoplume, neat to the barbs, which

I feel, feel sharply, keenly, ever so precise.
While I pick poses on the pink, his birds

expose rainbows, of all colours, and fill
the freighted air

VI.

Not a feather but it speaks, speaks pure *pipiare*.
Out, in the world's whirl and *erleben*.

And whereas I have learnt this bird, this here,
this here; have learnt its wink and blink,

its telling cock and crook, tucked leg all
bumbled up and cooked in avitrol;

you, quite casually, have struck
a natural attitude, more vivid and more

volatile, quick to the life in-coming. And,
pecked down to the dust and dirt, more free.

Here is the puff and bow and flirt, the
pirouette and turn, hop up and turn, the

turn and screw, weight rocked back, riskily,
weight thrown back, clean to the cloaca.

Soft in my margins, from a thudded gutter
– whispering a warm goodnight – jumps

one bird's last gapes, her dying prattle,
of long purples lain in her lap, her breath

pumped from her panting plump, as-if as-if
it matters

VII.

This one's for remembrance, then, old mole:
I'm stood at the corner of Sweet Lady,

the Pau Gargallo, Wash Lane, and Penfold,
where the two thousand sad souls go,

off on their over-rounds, bursting for
their Polish day trips, all on eggshells,

and the others – forty thousand brothers,
and a few lost sons – parade down around

the rosemary-scented lanes. *For you.* I'm
down by the bookies, in my scarlet anorak,

and good jeans, gone to your gamblers,
to lay some old depending debts, and still

still scratching in silver as I cross your path
saying '*pyggion,*' *sotto voce,* as I go about

my business, past some soon, some dead,
some dying squib. Damp in the guttering.

This time I step aside, to let an old man of Daulis
pass, this time

VIII.

Pichón, pijon, paloma. A little late, I've come
down, to let my self out, to pass the time

among the haunts – *how pale they glare –*
on just an off-chance, just a longing shot,

that you're still here, between the lines,
walking through our sentences, in piles of such,

between the street lamps, gas lamps,
Clayton's spirits, everything upright and waiting;

I walk the run perspectives, ribbon down
from the church of the Madeleine, all the way

to rue Montmartre, shining in the arc-glass and
réverbère with such clarity; I look for you,

white and pure, in the reverb air, buried
in the squeaking grass, the lamp-lit stacks,

asking, *how strong is stillness?* And I'm back
in the garden, in clouds of gnats, quietly

conning you, old owl, and knowing you
by my shadow, by the rustling of paper

and a hundred good hellos. Knowing, by your
lustre and your rigmarole. So frame that.

Perhaps I'm here – here, in a sort – and opened
up indirectly to confront such things, to pay

out keen attention, as my complex feet send
out their *tentif* towlines and I'm locked

to your stance, all pigeon-toed, dove-tailed.
What happened – *da!* – to my best prime object?

What happened – *da!* – to the writhes
of Ophelia, next? What happens then, if I fetch you?

Bundled up, among the broken mirrors,
you rage for it, everywhere in flair.

Bearded up, bound about among the
compound compliment, the breaking mirrors,

found to be all-one in the shifting change,
charged in your den, your lair, your pen. I swear,

I'll take the brushes, wrapped up, screwed,
screwed in your bedclothes and kind obituaries,

take too your palette, so subdued and so
deep layered despite its razor trim; sure,

I'll swipe a canvas where and when I may,
with your thick-skinned oils, acrylics,

all dried celedon, all egg-yolk yellows, reds
going black, blues going back, pinch by pinch,

Light Hooker's green, a core of cobalt,
hemmed in pinked lining, and very grey.

But it's all still yours, still yours to say, José,
of all the very this, this much is more.

I'm just a passing cyclist leaning on a pillar,
face turned to such a morning light,

among the rosy pink. I'm well outlined, here,
played out against the bright work, just

playing happy pigeon, playing pigeons
in your cold form plastic guttering; I'm

under your flash line and trapping chantlate,
tapping at the ogee eavestrough, rapping

its black fascia bowl, to hear how well it
rings

Tact

By the privy entries of the eare,
words sappe downe
into the heart, and,
with gunshotte of affection,
gaule the mind,
where reason and virtue
should rule the roste.

FIRST REPETITION

Immediately so
and so as palm to palm
do our kind contracts kiss.
Immediately to
intergraft in such soft contacts,
tact to tact
skinful of our fuss
of warm brushed haptic.
Immediately by
hap to hap contracted
to our eyes' kiss.
Unmediate.

SECOND REPETITION

If I could lap myself
up tight so tight to
you, we (you and I)
could crush out and.
If I could lap us
tight so to we you I

would crush out
first person
personal.
If lap us
tight we
crush.

THIRD REPETITION

Need no postman for
each hap riposte; need
no interim parcel
force; need no parole patrol;
no punctuating drum;
nor nurse; nor Friar Peter;
need no re-prefix as we fine flex
ply taut cord petition, storing places
membering port to post
signed to it. Turn and turned again,
bound to the turn and turn.
Nobody interfering, over here.

FOURTH REPETITION

To touch: to move or grieve; to
come; to deceive;
to quip; to taunt; to take up; to
write; to speak,
or mention a thing.

FIFTH REPETITION

To be sent back
I step back
make room back up
push space to stare
slot intervals interim
a mediating as we
throw out into a busy medium.
The bounce between us
links out lovely chain
causal interactions hot
on heels, lagging cause to
overlapped event, coat over coat
laid out and over. Without the
gap, perhaps we can't
get intimate.
You snap distinct only
on the far side of
a mediating tumble.

FINAL REPETITION

And are the ethics of adoration that
I stand far back enough to stare?
Listening intently behind the closed door
to you to you as you.

{{ *du* | *he* | *tao* }}

I.

In the Linshui marketplace,
you stand among rows
of shell on shell:
trying to make
a chance.

Tap: just when I'm all hulled up
all crabbed in confine
comes your unexpected
crick and nap and crack,
smart sound of tough love
on my round nutshell,
the flex and squeezed pop
of steely hap-crackers
snapped on infinite space.

Your husky insinuations
tend to my shelly cave;
you apply your callipers
and the heartnut aches.

You ground around it
lick soft sound
right round it
give lip up down it:
you take your breaks,
make flouts and entry-touts,
flushed over and out
quite tight to the fine fractures.

II.

Fetch Felix with all his nine lives!
Here comes the Radical Squad:
Trojans on their
long walk.

Tap: you side-step
racked hair-triggers,
drip-lines, trip-
wire now silly-strung

all green–lit, defused
overlines out across
my active areas: and so
no bang, no bang.

III.

With ink from crushed walnuts,
he drew a foetus in utero,
and studies of birds:
'if there is no love,
what then?'

Groan us quite together
tight till pips speak;
grind to find the
white sincerity
of sliced bread-and-butter.

Sure, there is a kernel of some
mattered thing
in here and understood
if only you can eat it
and make it matter much.

Every tale, told to tend;
every seed, on-the-nail,
palpably pecked
just so
remotely touched.

Your smoothed ectoderm
moves between my hushed lips
my chapped seams;
your horn bill chirrups,
demand response,
insisting payment, up and out,
my brain-pan cleft by a brown bill.

Passerine, push your bills your rosters
clear under the door
sealed in soft keratin.

So slip your keen rostrum
through my outer wall:
tap tap, rat–a–tat.

IV.

A man's house is his castle
and each man's home,
his safest refuge,

Click-click come release
my high-sprung tender chords,
my tight-strung relockers;
scoping out the change
scooping up the charge
with your sure fingers
touching tumblers – T5 to T8 –
tripping notches on the sternum
so so sensitive to
sleight slops in my spun dials.

Peeling back drop-locks
– pericardium through epicardium –
stripping out clocks
– myocardium through endocardium –
unshackling each blocked valve
with one eye keyhole clamped
one tip pushing whorls
through ventricle and hardplate.

Twenty-one thousand nervous times
or seventy-two times per minute
is all in all it takes
on autodial
and I'm outstunned

hot-lanced on such hot thermals
such hot *vena cava* such hot chordae.

And if all else fails
take this safe
take this heart
and just
bounce it
all the way
down stairs.

That should flick the trips
turn tricks, click clicks.

V.

so particular and
so tender.

O, O, O, Peterman,
although I'm glad to see you
doing your job,
you beak intruder,
you superthief, you
barefoot dinnertime bandit,
don't think on a white instant
that I don't apprehend you,
loafing around, stealing about,
pilfering the shopfloor
of Bertha's Gift & Home Furnishings,
violin under one arm,
and *Tete de Femme*, the other.

I left the door ajar,
broken for entry,
predisposed
for your hot-prowl,

for your calling card
on my welcome-mat.

VI.

-sh | -shh | -shhh | -shhhh
no words, no words
hush hush
-sh

Tap tap: as Bourne-shell shifts
on crushed Korn-shell
as softly C-shells born
again to Bash, and
as the grit gets in
clean through
clear to
the snagged heartstone,
I dare to hope you may
just see
it's me | concisely.

Shortcut to me
shortcut sent to you
in a shared moment
of sheer felicity,
spliced standard-to-offbeat,
dragged out along
my leading edges
across platforms
into new contexts
and laid out
relational.

VII.

Give me that man and I will
wear him at heart's core
in my heart of heart

Until at last, with apple pie,
with plum pudding,
and eye-spy-glass,

as I do thee:

hush

cased up *hús*
in their paper bag,
you came clean
to the little house
to its open door,
to tease the drawback
to cut the head
to part the charge,

    the hot cloud
    the hot cloud
    the hot crowd of
    thermal swarmed electron
    of eased atomic orbital
    in gradient still and
    radiating

Sweet remnant,
wear right through
the core-wall,
hold fast to
the heart of hearts
– *au cœur du corps* –
dismantle, drill,
go crash go dump,
and strip back insulation
to take each cord and twist

    each threaded twine
    each high-fibered hawser-line
    teased out on the heartrope
    scoped tight to find
    the red electric
    ravelling

VIII.

Alone in the Linshui market,
and whistling to the air,
Lin Changzhu is out
among the ranks
of shell and
shell and
shell:
you pays,
you takes your
choice, your chance

Du he tao: we're out here
just betting on skin.

Come, slice right though it —
cute through cupule —
and let's see what we've got.

I'm all out here: gambling.

An English walnut or *nux Gallica*?
mopan-mopan or mother-child?
a dud, a duff? dog-throw ratscrew
slapjack snap (tap-tap)
a right fine pair.

This one: a government official's hat,
a chicken's heart, a lantern: that.

And you're twisted in
doubled up, front-run vigorish
for the vulture or the Venus throw:
skin in the game, pounds of it.

Now on the nutshell
stick the knife-drop on
capsule's tender acupoint,
clip point to the tense yield strain
to track tip through
hawkpoint keen to kerf
and trailing
wanton slipped swarf
in surfy cream curls
and open out and out and up:
and there

it's me

sat with a crimped copy of Homer,
and a lucky cricket.

I am, it seems, rolled round
palmed around
worth the punting
gambolled smooth
all good in circulation
just hap and unconfined:
nothing to be
frayed by.

IX.

So with one finger, press-by-press,
arm stretched out of bed,
I type up slow happen-
stance on keywater
brightboarding

while you
sleep

Divided-back

I.   *I shall be*   *under the clock...*

Right away,   we meet
in   white frame,
on   bright borders,
cut cute   to the divided-back.

We block out   Big Letters,
pressed on   large linen,
in   Victorian lilac, or green issue,
in all these   impermanent pigments.

This   by-the-seaside smut –
two pints of stout   and donkey ride touts –
is only sent   to strangers. But
by the by, I do   wish you were here.

Such   sinister design, such rich figment,
when held up to   hard light,
reveals   no secrets here:
just quick scrawls   in empty places.

Just   unstopped write-aways,
dashed open   in post-haste spaces,
traced   in double-impress trawls,
to drop-sink, and fall   slick in fugitive ink.

And as each card,   every envoy, fast tracks out
impossible   synchronicities,
it trawls   and tries, and tries to syncopate,
crawls back   on the tight off beat.

There are   it says
no hidden things   it says
                     in this corner
                     of the human heart.

II.   *I must*   *remember...*

No hidden things   then
tucked out   stuck out
and up   in plain view

each card   can't come
but comes   by bit by bit
coming   closer to contact

so sticks the wall   to hide
quite   out of sight
in sight   and over seen

the most observed   of all
that passes show   and so
each   squinting overseer

whose inky hands   riffle
through all   the cheeky orisons
the   cheque-stubbed countersigns

through   dead letter drafts
those ghosts   that spook the post
those   undelivered bills unanswered

whose finger   tips to tip in
tea leaves' tips and apple peel
touch to tip whose   thumbs thumb

33

whose index whorls   skip
and tremble   over and over each and
rifle through   each squared off surface

each planed view   tipping off
ticking over   each gridsquared
turn by turn   and turn again

to find   pinched postcards
replaced   to place
to wish you here   *grus aus*

to hide   gently foxed
in plain sights
side to side

so that

     would scan
and   sound out

safe   it says
and

     sound.

I really
     must stop…
It says.   *I really must.*

III.   *It struck me*   *rather forcibly…*

Once they've   ruined my upholstery,
will they

     leave us alone?

Now that each cushion   is needled, and every
chair leg and desk top   scoped out,
                               is the observation over?

                    You   though,
                    you sit   behind green glasses, your soft eyes
                               green glancing.

          And you can   softly see.
                  And   seek, and sift, and sort.
          And you can   gently take what they mistake.

I didn't hide it,   so you couldn't find it.

Come round   for your snuffbox.
Let me be distracted   by gunshots
in the street.

                               I want you to switch
                               what I sealed and signed.

          I didn't hide it so you couldn't find it.

IV.   *Sorry,*   *I couldn't get away…*

I envelop you   in penny postcards
so loud and clear   so no one
no one sees   sees fit to intercept to flick
to flick   to switch the finger
to finger   point to point
to post to post   to say out loud
so no one sees   to hear the ear.

35

Put it up!   Put them up!

You dupes   you post officers
you highwaymen you   envoys you
Poins you Prince   you Dupin Turpin
you all will miss   the post the kiss
the mark the open   I love you
and   I didn't hide it
there are   no secrets here
the overt   I love you
there are   no hidden things
the plain   I love you
here   and here
                      where anyone can see
                      if looking
                      liking moves.

Argus Panoptes

I.

Stay a wide awake
with each of all
your hundred eyes
      amazing:
each shot rod
is just so hot
and every dazzled cone
      is blazing.

Don't let the short-sights,
those over-lookers in.

You will be gaoler;
you will be him.
You can keep me, free
from irreversible trim.

II.

Look, see, think in key:
I'm out on wing
in your gym, where
every enthralled gesture,
every turn of captivated
limb on limb and limb,
each fallen flower at my feet
(networks of
      laylock,
      lilaz,
      nilak,

little violent rhomboids all)
should still be noticed,
still be taken down,
still be ambushed,
            noted and denoted.
Curve the key
            elliptic
to tether our covert days
to your uptorn olive tree,
and turn me out,
torn forward to a future.

Just don't let back
            a green past,
a cage-glazed echo
of dirty-white flowers,
the sound of savage lilacs
            not loud or long,
the horns and motors
            burning
            ai ai
            burning
down mid-green lanes.

III.

I'm all panned-out,
crow-toed,
a rogue grown honest:
            dazed
in the prison gym,
to be tucked in
down on your M Cells,
snug tight in P Cells,
bright lit in K Cells,

so sensitive
so switched saccadic.

Under the carbon arcs,
Mangin mirrors and Leigh lights
– all eyes, no sight –
nobody spots
my scattered iridescence
        pluming
        in parabolas
through concertina wire,
        blooming
on each cold-crimp.

IV.

And, blind in the hot gaze
of our artificial moonlight –

        bulb-blind to the twisting lumens,
        the threaded candles,
        as each affective bright beam,
        in all its volting incandescence,
        hits our ignite-strike
            our magnet-hum
        to spill, spin, and rift,
        out adrift from our corona
        in filigree in filament
            in slender air –
          so slender & white,
          so solide & strong –

and nobody notes
        this wild

    this
incoherent spin.

V.

Wax-faced, hay-stuffed,
I'm still sat still
in the back
behind ballistic-glass –
that flexes
not to shatter –
    drinking wine,
      eating crisps,
teaching you chess,
foreplay, and harpsichord.

Make one last cast
    one call
    and call;
I'm just sewing postbags here
– stitching gapes and eyebores –
just doing the gaoler
doing the gaoler
in a hundred
    hushed voices.

VI.

Yes, you know they'll come,
to try their luck, and leave –
    so duck it
    weave it.
Sharp cattle-rustlers, drivers
disguised as sheep-herds –

all so very keen
to give you one
damn good crack.

In He comes, wings buzzing,
gadding from his arras,
out from the black room,
the wind-beaten crossroads,
waltzing in to set
his strict intercept –
all slick quicksilver –
     buzz buzz
all head and beard and balls.

He'll try to catch us,
     buzz buzz
plucked clean, right
from the drossy interim:
he aims to arrest us; prick us out;
by opening our post;
steaming open aerograms,
with searches and seizures;
scrawling our blanks;
each pocket picking;
resigned, resealed,
and undelivered.
     Buss buss

Here He comes,
     buss buss
excellent in all his tricks
till the cool stainless spring
rushes in the hinge.
Till *sessho-seki*, killing stone
snake-egg hag-stone hits,
cures you, clean between the eyes.

And the blood rush
stings.

The *bringer of luck.*
The *guide and guardian.*
Murderer.

VII.

My love, you best keep wide
        – awake –
among their boring stories
with all your hot hundred
dazzling
            open eye-balls
                    alert
                    and
                    all
                    amazing.

Eurydice in Euston Square

I.

Perhaps you heard of
      how we left them

        rapt and blown and
bound to forget fleetwater;

of how deftly dumbstruck,
      tranced by my song

of kiss and burning,
      long loss and turning,

        they hot to this,
in sweetest over–awe;

or perhaps you heard
      of how, in tears

and so furiously wet
      with tears and tears,

        they cede a reweave
for your recent ghost;

how gold gold Proserpina
      permits a soft requick'ning.

The all, I ask,
is to enjoy it;

                    the all I ask
                 of you is that.

But my eye turns
                 to hold, be held,

and, right on edge
                 of the brightest world,

                        you slipped
                 off on their atmosphere;

and you complain, then,
                 spinning out and out,

           and faintly you complain,
that you were loved.

Flipped from each string,
                 each spandrel to spring

                 off stairways, so trim
                        to the thin air

II.

And yet, there must
                 have been some time

                 for look-back then;
when I glanced you,

who simply came away –
                 adrift on every escalator –

                    slipped off from each
hot-step, tripped off

by your dimly falling.
                    Why did you go

when I'm still calling
                    out for full recall?

                    When did you go,
cartwheeled from the riser?

Clipped from metallic trim,
                    cut clean from stringers,

there must have been
                    some split quick trim

                    turned up and over
on the strip-lit stairs

                    that flipped the tack,
tripped the switchback back,

                    as you just tumbled
                    apart on the stairwell.

                    Oh, how you tumbled
                    bright from your paternoster

                    reversing wet fence rolls
right back into underground.

III.

I don't know when
            I looked to lose

you, or heard you
            spiralled off on spindrift.

                        I know I must
have looked long on

            the concrete corner for
that high electric kiss,

                        your hand to push,
hard to the plasticoat,

                        warm to the blue,
rich in corporate colour,

                        for your hip suede
tough to this handrail

            tough touch and urgent
at all 600 surgence.

I'm still stood there,
            really, in the residue,

                        really, on the echoes,
                        really, all the traces.

Sometimes just simply say
            I will keep looking

back on moments, just
for volts and heartbeats.

The curved spine and
eye and hook and

arching red laced hits
by bright hairfall, brightening.

The hipbone bevel and
roughly took and hotly

thrown out: best sight
of my whole life.

IV.

No great take, then,
that I looked for

all the eyes dazzle
and therefore lost it.

Come back up stairs,
bring your brush back,

your startling skin fuss,
your every amazing rush.

Come back up stairs,
bring back my words,

my sharp line flush
on you, to us.

Come back with our
                    sad songs all winter,

                    and don't repent an
over-elaborate alphabet spent

                    on your inner thigh,
        touched to soft us.

Come back up stairs
                        if you read me

                        up in the subway
missing the tube travel,

missing the coach trips,
                    all the seaside rides,

the telephones, the postcards,
                    telegrams on spun wire;

come back up stairs,
                    and I'm hanging on

                    subjunctives, hanging on
                    superlatives, hanging on

the sound of someone
                    long gone to static

V.

And now then – now
                    and then – I'm just

                    back up and out
alone in the stairwell,

whistling Dixie – away, away –
                    walking up and around

and around down there
                    on the clinker stair,

                    blinking in mine eyes'
dazzle. Left to wonder

when I shot it
                    when I slipped it

when it all went
                    down, put down to

                    chits of ecstasy, slipped
memorial bits, filed away

                    as cracked mishits, so
sloughed so cold to

                    such cold storage, so
ripe for your re encryption.

Sometimes your warm breath
                    seems just so tight

just seems so tight
                    to my up-turned collar;

                    at times you come
                    so near that I

          almost think that near
on heal I hear

     your humming your hemming
behind as you're coming

in kind, up close,
               with your closing footfall

               tight to the gathering
glare, ripe for one

          preposterous stare, but you're
not there, not there

               where I missed you
off, kissed off into

blue-iced dioxide air, the
               stalled carbonic, the stalling

               there, as you cartwheel
off down Euston Square

               lost to the gritgrey
of every Portland stair

                    and falling. And,
in every grasp and grab

               my hands miss you.
And my mouths, grabbed,

my tongue, grabbed, my
grabbed blindfolded fingers, are

all, all too, of

how to miss you

Pentimenti

I.

So, trickster, there I am, tucked into the grass
for you to glance at behind flat glass.

So, saboteur, there we are, sunk knee-deep in the inch-thick,
fat to the gummy wooze, made up full in the facture

while each eye draws to the door, while every eaves-
dropper snugs chop-chop to the rafters.

We are at one jump, one kick beyond the ordinary.
We are at jump, *right to it*: fingers loved in the colour tone;

fists tight to the high thrum; limbs lain twist in the warp,
in, at the first weave

                  stitched   and oh-so starkly starkly
           without a dry thread on.

II.

I'm going further in among black orchids,
among black hyacinths, lurking in the opacity

of an overgrown orchard, snapping into our
interminable débris of revision

                 sinking
                     into the underdrawn.

You – soft between the dials and tentive to the redials –
slipped me soft off hook, switched clear off a clean step,

and left me lost out here – dialling, dialling – left me
out of each and every key exchange, to loop and loop

through each of every bad bad branchline's reach.
So wrung out rung in starkstruck reroute right round

such nerve-taut tough telephonics, O, such livewire centres,
O, such rough rate centres, such awesome plugboard din.

III.

And so, this should be seen as all wild-eyed in capped careen
unhushed, and come as a desperate dive, a last gasped finely final call

        – falling galled appalled –
in dumb steamed crambo – as comeback come back please:

           as
           one for the road.

But this then stands around like a late careering, hit
against hope: a shot sliced askance to the fine grain; adrift

to the rainfall, just a doe-struck call-back reeling back,
back to the clumsy couch, to hot drops on the plastic roof –

        just crude flesh and hipbone, back to rude things,
                that mattered: raw things, lost.

IV.

What, so I'm grown so tonedeaf in ringdown? What,
so I'm so lost in switch, so lost so lost to the patchcord crossfire

that you slip the ringing cord, that you drop the rear cord
slot to the hot electric jack — and there, among sharp static,

this buzzbell and fedback feedback fuzz that I'm calling?
                                        Out in the wire world.

Your lips, step out of cinch, broke clinch, but I mouth around
                        for our lovely wordstuff.

Dialled right on up to the cool-blue booty. Keeled right up and up
            to your hot neon-tips, your hot fluorescent, that peels off

among these screeds, and ravelling ravelling under their radars,
                        off from their cold cut tenderhooks;

the one last peaky tentation cast off in-coming kiss-me-quick
raiders homing in, in stealthy for even such an even-chance

    of such a hot
                                        catch-up.

Of those from the ships

A sequence

Ptolemaeus the king of Egypt was so eager to collect a library, that he ordered the books of everyone who sailed there to be brought to him. The books were then copied into new manuscripts. He gave the new copy to the owners ... but he put the original copy in the library with the inscription 'of those from the ships.'

GALEN

I. Of those from the ships

So you can come along and you can scan it:
come along the docks, as are your curious customs,
and you can move among my spread
among my freight my cargo.
And you should catch a draft to drift
to drift from crate my love to crate
my love through freight my lovely argosy.

So you can leaf your dusty tips through wheat and chaff
and riffle out each inky index
through all the silken slough
of all my gaudy textiles.
Flick through it, resort it, recall it
to recount and to your count enlist
my disembarked, my unencrypted holdings.

And so, ascribe each part, just so,
inscribe each piece, just so,
describe each Hippocrene flask, just so,
each cask, just so: of all my all content.
To each a place in place to place
in your exact accountant call
of row by rolling row anatomies.

Now as you go, steady
my dizzying inventories, steady
my whole to holed in hold and steady as you go.
Until amongst the richer sort, my finer stuff,
my love, my weft, my warp, my woof, my loom,
you come across, you chance upon
my books, my textured library.

Like Antony, enlisting scrolls for Egypt,
I've weighed up with ranks of primed romance,
rows of charged letters, waxed flattery.
Please read them quick; respond at length but
on the instant, as each squeezed line tips
tight up on the grazed edge, squeaks 'come!'
and soft speaking means the softly same.

Pinched, each plundered volume plumbs
your depths of cheek of face of front.
The bitter gall of it, from row to row
shelf to shelf and decimal point to point.
You and your low-toned underlings, *sotto voce*,
unstack, stack up, pack up and off
with those, all those from my ships.

Your tough customs, your officious vandals,
all horn-rimmed reading glasses
and hob-nailed boots spectacular
along my aisles, through my stacks,
and scrawling down my gangplanks.
So silence please. And no talk back to back
to no recourse to no redress to silence please.

You rogue librarian, filling packing cases;
you rough justice, packing shipping crates;
you vile bibliophile, stealing a borrow;
you unrepentant lovely lender.
Fingered, found red-handed
shameless-faced, each fly defaced:
of those – you wrote – *from the ships.*

You with their hollow whispers
of silenced, pleased apology
towing away my textures
of those from the ships

You book thieves pirates book robbers;
you book thieves collectors borrowers lovers
of those from the ships

Of course, I knew your Alexandrian law.
I knew you'd come, and knew you'd take them.
Of course, I brought along my best materials –
first editions, originals, manuscripts –
and must have hoped you'd steal them.
This is the hope, of course off course,
of all those from such a stricken ship

of all those from the ships.

II. Don't see, don't hear, don't speak

Up in accessions – pens poised – scribes sit:
licked tips, knibs crooked like parrots,
rawly tattering with their tawny bills,
giving thumb-nail nips with their monkey fingers
(here comes one who looks merrily methinks –
frisking his Feathers, cocking his Nib).
Dim drums throbbing, down halls half heard.

They've been waiting weeks: hanging about,
making fly-catch mouths, picking fleas from fur,
husking coffee, scratching bum notes, prepping pages,
rehearsing: deliver the stillborn calf by Monday;
make membrane; dip soak in vats of calcium hydroxide,
lime and caustic water; then dry chalk shake off.
Your walls are hung with palatine velum, black and soft as sin.

They took each skein of silken skin unscudded –
pulled taut in the herse from wet to dry,
its texture tight from pebbled eyelet hooklet –
amazed, astonished, bleached, and pumice-stoned,
struck scraped *lunarium* on uterine vellum.
Your imitative mystic apes, your writing types, all readied:
these Don Johns of Alexandria are going to the war.

In that enormous silence, Britches stitches up his eyes,
Moneke whirls a tip to plug an ear (no news from Gordo),
as they await receipt of all your recent re-acquisitions.
The bookish beaked impressionist troop, perched, hushed, waits.
Blank slates stand smooth and even clean from Nibs and Lustre.
How now they hold up cleft nebs, hold up cleft quill to you, and
now, in that enormous silence, comes the noise of your Crusade.

Noise of books coming from the barks, *bóc, béce, bók*, beech to beach,
and riding up and over from Alexandrian docks
— all love-light woven of sunset sunlight and seas —
and along a winding road, rolls each pinched book on book,
and then the tuckets, then the trumpets cannon, and then they come:
boxes full of tangled things and texts for aching eyes,
of *liber* stock disembarked, redrafted from my emptied crafts.

Now. Accessions comes to life, inspired alight, quick flared,
no reservations, no preserved stock, no locked shelving now.
One prehensile pygmy takes his pick, lick lips his digit,
takes-up, checks-out the way of things, cracks spine, begins:
Of those, he enscripts, *from the ships*. Meticulous mimic.
And now the green eyes flip and flit, from manuscript to script:
my Venus, Goddess, my daedal Divine, so flee, so smile and glow.

And across the aisle — two rows up, one to the side — his mate,
who murmurs soft, that none can hear the sorrow of his heart, no longer waits.
And now — humile, modest snitches all — *the savage beasts begin to play.*
Now. It's in the air: cadent type, descending minims, procreant atoms,
textual primal matter, primal seeds of primal lettered things.
Your pauper-speech, purloined, must find strange terms
to fit — *why then, I'll fit you* — the strangeness of these things.

Around the reading room, spectacled secretaries unfurl my loving scrawl,
to decipher my character from all two hundred thousand scrolls.
While down in your archives, Mizaru's cameo, all blind stamp and punch:
rolling carnelian seals in wet clay, pushing amethyst in hot wax.
Silently secreted in maps and manuscripts, Mikazaru cuts in deep relief:
inks heights, plumbs depths, and, under his soft papillary impress,
he figures forth our secrets. *Of those*, is his incision, *from the ships.*

For ten quarters of a century, immutable Mazura — placed among rare books,
humming among music — has kept his iron plate hot, ready
set for this action, and now he goes, blocks out, fills out the forms,
serries solid ceramics, tables these motions, these movable sullied types.

And Shizaru, your overseer – often overlooked – covers his cock,
inspects the substrate stocks, the typographic blocks,
scans a golden eye over casts, smoke proofs, moulds and matrices.

Your dear and tender monkeys second-guessed each stanza,
in accuracy they never broke my scene, interleaved or intervened;
your fifteen talented copyists, erotic secretariat,
your book-loving mechanicals, weave my own dreams.
Your copyists they gently took me down, they surely shook me,
down from off my shelf, and dusted down my jacket sleeves,
stood all on point, all pricked out, and punctuated the spliced grammar

of all those from the ships.

III. In fire-ships

So that: I have I think she said out-wearied my welcome.
We have she said she thinks assumed too long.
And so, I – prolonged from berth, pulled from your bay –
and so I – launched from your broiling docks,
parsing from our to mine to me, passing from us to I from we,
drawing out on heavy oars, off beats and up and down and
suffering long drawn-out departure – am held off in thinning air.

Up led, I have presumed to long – too long too long – to long.
So depart yourselves ANCHORS UP PLEASE and off this time:
anchors, pulled to purchase, apart a-weigh a-peak a-trip apart,
and – *O may my fathomed heart burst from breast-lock* –
hoist hard from the cap. Sheet it hard home. Trim it and ready it.
Until, tongue-tied, tack paid, tack struck and pulled apart,
I'm sent out all discomposed, edged out in surgent underways.

Head to the wind, I hurry out across your silted bay –
all choked up on our remnant paper scraps, book deposits,
with our off-cut fragments, our discard chits, our chats and pieces –
my soothed passage all impeded by unexpedited piles
of unedited recollection, built-up weeds, and shored-up ruins.
My oars pull such hard distance, against such tightened thread,
such uncompassionate umbilical, hard plucked to twitch too taut.

And every silver stroke – a tender rebuke, a lover's pinch – doubles
our heavy freighted interim, doubles redoubles at a stroke
and now – soft now – I am soft struck with soft sorrow.
Care renewed, sorrow renewed, wearily awake: I am sent out.
Here. Over the binding of the waves. Fleeting.
I'm cursing your clumsy cartographers. Feeling the gap.
I'm swearing on smudged stenography. Minding the gap.

Here, as I move across Great Harbour, all around me burning fleet;
all about about our reel and rout, Egypt's boats and bridges burn.
Her barges boil the water in satiating splendour of blazed bark.
Her barges burn upon the water. Burnt green and blue and white.
From up cloud-high, raised waves stoop up and down
to cuff craft in brackish foam, as aerial sparks skip
ship to ship, mast-point to point in violet *Corpo Sancto*.

In the waist now, now on the deck, in every cabin now,
inflamed amazement flames distinct, now meets and join.
And looking back on consternated docks, your first responders
– all tooled up too hot with their spreaders, cutters, rams –
get frantic to isolate each incident ecstatic ember:
rushing to tamp down my insatiate cormorant heat my heart;
rushing to peninsulate against my rash my fiercest blazings.

I dream that down Pudding Lane to St Paul's, stones fly grenado,
that melting lead runs streets in streams, too hot for horses' hooves;
I dream that down in crypt your printers await their conflagration.
'Pish,' you mutter, 'a woman could piss it out'
but you're sound drowned out by powder kegs, exploding in your kremlin.
And perhaps, with your face in the wind, you are burned
with a shower of firedrops. O the ecstatic the calamitous spectacle.

Too late, your bills and hooks plunge in thatched charcoal.
'It makes me weep,' perhaps you'll say, 'to see it.'
But know this: it wasn't Caesar who fired your fleet. So lock your doors.
It wasn't some pagan-fearing patriarch, or some caliph,
who broke down your walls. So look to your books.
It's my eyes' dazzle in the flames' reflect, spitting hot spirit;
my twisted thread of kindred fire so fleet from fleet to kindle.

Best wake Tesibius – give him stir – who slept through his alarm,
to damp down the up in air pumped plumes, my doting volatiles.
Best pay Crassus and his full five hundred who loiter in the smoke.
Bellman, call out the fair Pi Kappa Alpha, your chaste watermen!

Alert your inexpressive vigilantes! Let slip the blind, the gouty dalmatians!
But, did I burn even your first defences, or skip a single crennelation?
Did my sparks ever truly fly from eye to eye? And, did you even catch it?

From high up on Palatine or Esquiline, you watch boats sweetly sink;
and, serene from mighty strife, your fingers suspend on heartstrings.
While everywhere, disaster averted, the flames deaded-down extinguish
utterly. You wouldn't even know it happened, if indeed it did.
Some soft god of pleasure has broken his bow, put out his light
and turned out the lights. There are no fire-ships in this harbour.
Perhaps there never were. And I'm mere-weary now: now I know it.

You told me, don't look back to shore as shore recedes,
but I'm sore sure astonished, robbed of air at my rude departure –
wood within breathless wood – so much amazed – I know not what.
Hands on the deck deal out extended clewline, *chordae tendineae.*
Perhaps we were the good *per se*, and won't be found again.
Buntline, papillary leechline, runs out through deadeyes.
We were perhaps the good itself, and won't be found again.

So, down in the hold my dizzied stock-keeper counts the cost,
Inventories what's not, sub-divides our bill, checks an addition,
but can't quite account a sense of abstract loss.
Sure, all the books are here; their secret dedications all intact.
Remembrances turned safe back by sender. Present, and correct.
Calf-skin spines, gold-leaf lettering, all as in the catalogue, all as-is,
so nobody would scan and note the swap the switch, the brilliant exchange

of all those from the ships.

IV. *Rete mirabile*

And now the restless man awakes
out beyond the harbour wall
plunged by wake washed conduit
bathed interlaced in channels
involved among their flow and spread
of cadent fall and fret and runnel
of giddy net and saturated space.

[*I wake unfolded out*
over twenty-one square foot of deck
each cutaneous square inch
a thousand-fold of nerve
still sensible to a long extended press;
your still, your lucid touch prolonged
through corneum, lucidum, basale]

Go give the care-held keel a kick;
set rank to signal breakers now.
Dig the heel to catch careen on roll
along about the reel the stagger
tossed and scattered. Torn to tatters.
'I'm far away out here,' I said.
Inside your dazzling influences.

[*You sloughed clean through*
thirty dead cell layers
– the basal lamina
insular epiderm –
imprinting tense connection
deep in the elastic heart
through reticule and papillæ]

I am out along electric clamour,
among swan's song translated
into a swan's cry, a swan's blare,
in the dull distort of gull music
(but 'lah-di-dah,' is all they say)
and still my mews' song sounds
loud around the gulls' mewling.

   [*depth projected through*
   scarf skin gloss skin
   to kiss off this true-skin.
   Mine corium my derma:
   you inscribed upon the underside
   with careful impress:
   all mine from the ships]

And so caught out in stormy weather
the grand mystery of flux & reflux,
the flowing and ebbing of the sea
my mind gets blown by aggregate emotion
by vigorous simpathetical connexions.
Streams, it seems, do entwine with streams.
And lakes do twist with lakes.

   [Touché, *you touched the nerve net,*
   tocca, *hit homing over canal and cleft*
   along the plate and groove through glue
   to toc *down on the synapse, axons, radials:*
   those inside dazzling influences
   those mesenteric sympathetic plagues from
   fibers felt down dear, down down in the gut]

Nothing to say about my self
as simply complete:
or intermingled admixture.
Nothing of concrete self to say

the one way or the other.
So much of me was in the interim,
and that much left around your library.

[*Go open your eardrum. Obey, and be attentive.*
Tease out integrity along this feeling line.
Impact me out, redound me: beat
tender integers, and make me unintact.
Down me soundly each tendon unbound me
wholly; fractional; entirely; touched till taut.
Go list, lean in: I barely am intact. I barely am.]

I turn the ear. Hope for feedback.
Tacit *ishin-denshin*, dear System I.
I turn the ear. Catch only tenor,
sound of stretching oars extending,
the fed-back beat, the stroke, beat, stroke;
catch curlew's calls through spindrift,
crying: *what, then, has god wrought*

of those from the ships?

V. Call signs: Morse

Each morning before dawn
I'm on the wireless with inaudible murmurs
in-calling OLD MAN TO YOUNG LADY
in dots dashed tapped out
in railroad code – dah-di-dah-dah –
in blinking torture – dah-di-dah-di-dah –
in click and sigh and real catastrophe.

Calling you: THIS IS MY LAST CRY
BEFORE ETERNAL SILENCE.
For no high-keyed reply. For no remorse.
Three dots, three dashes, then three dots.
The stylus is caught up static, unimpressed.
So then, consign it, call it, sign it off with:
just a single strike, a dit, a signature dot.

Late morning, I'm licking stamps,
writing wish-you-were-here postcards,
and spelling out my signature address,
half enjoying my responsibilities.
I feel the pulled mute compulsion
of the tin-can telephone, of carriage bolts,
of teapot handles, and bustle wire.

Voice-like sounds trail in my wake
in tailed induction coil and liquid transmit
– epigraphs, epitaphs, blank embezzlings –
catching in the crosstalk and the hum,
as our parted pairing twines out across
an unbridgeable input-output chasm.
'Mr Watson – come here – I wont you.'

All these discontinuous waves:
all the engines of my ingenuity
can't help us now. By midday
I'm sounding hollow notes in bottles
and if I soon succeed I'll bask in glory,
shouting, 'Come here, all England confides!'
Calling, come here, unexpectant: I need you.

By evening, I'm posting pigeons
– my *cher ami* shot down in friendly fire:
your barrage is right on top of me!
please for heaven's sake stop it! –
I'm sending smoke alarms and semaphore
all one armed up and out. Help.
Romeo in approach at dip. Romeo close-up.

Juliet: I'm on fire with dangerous material;
keep well clear of me, my dear.
Uniform: I'm running into danger.
Delta: manoeuvring with difficulty.
Foxtrot: I'm disabled. Lima: quarantine me.
Victor, I need you. Kilo, I do. Zulu,
send your tugs. November in November.

At sunset, crack out red fusees
projectile flared pyrotechnic distress
in strontium nitrate sky lettering
in potassium nitrate picture postcards
I signal-bomb you up and over Yangzhou:
sawdust charcoal sulphur scrawling
of those from the ships scattered high.

And luminous calcium charges, depth-dropped,
catch pearls that were. Late at night: séances.
The Baron George and First Lady Lincoln
lay down their sly and shaky hands, but all we get
are Black Hawk, Pericles, Plato, Peter the Great,
just savages amassed in the medium. Not you.
Just dust and ashes on the spirit slate. Not you.

This correspondence, written at the moment
of our crash, goes unanswered quite.
Franz wrong. F wrong. Thine wrong.
They are for you, take them, take them again;
they kiss upon the wide hand in its delicate glove.
(She has made you write to yourself; she has made you
write; she made you; she has you; she has; you write.)

Not a word for a week. It really is dreadful.
I did get a telegram. But it wasn't meant
for me (my wise old woodland uncle wasn't 'of Milan').
Then, at last: 'We are sitting in the restaurant
at the zoo, after spending the afternoon sitting
in the zoo.' These are dreadful, wasted ecstasies,
failures to depart, lacking succession unsuspended.

Wrong! Wrong! Ghosts like ping-pong balls
move on between lines – perfidy! perjury! –
and written kisses won't reach their destination.
And neither (so, I know it now) does cross-eyed jealousy:
I best stop asking, 'Who is Herr Hartstein?
Who in hell he?' It is late. It is time. Stop, hap,
betimes to bed; with a good book from the ships …

and so, and there, 'tween my water-marked sheets
– tucked corners, crisp folds, mummy's linen –
I now discover the discrepancies, now the inky slips,
your monkey's inky pawprint, your misprints,
new mistranslations, mistranscriptions, variants,
sleight Egyptian encryptions. Each amazing errancy.
This is not my book: not one – and now it dawns –

of those from the ships.

VI. Call numbers: Dewey

Hulled down down haulage in amaze
– check titles, take stock, scan shelves –
all up put out and in exceeding maze
– inspect each copy, skim the reads –
all in wonder all in morning mist
– glance at, flick them, spot the swaps –
all wandering all evening all amaze.

You've switched my books. You've
purloined. Plainly. Is it possible? Is't
possible you rank abused my hospitality,
that you attempted such inelegant offence?
O royal knavery of ghastly bugs and goblins!
All subscribed, impressed, placed safely back;
all the changelings never known, unguessed. Till now.

Your happy hypocrites, these savage detectives,
have made their stealthy stacked assault, their
book attacks and hijackings to finger every packet
(and what books did these desperate men desire?).
I should charge you, bill you, hook you,
bless you, blow by hundred bamboo blows,
and break your inky blocks by blocks!

Where has my Hamlet gone along the Relativ Index?
He's run from 822.3 to 098 to sit among
prohibited books, forgeries, hoaxes.
Pamflets, notes, scrap books, *index rerums* move
out along the displaced decimals: 383
should be postal communication. But not of late.
Once, 387 was water transport. Attraction, 538.

Each faceted classification, cutter-numbered,
confound confused: no games of chance
at 795; no pulp and paper in the place;
no stars left among 500s; and 216 no longer used
(formerly Evil); 217 unassigned (formerly Prayer);
157 empty, formerly emotions; formerly will;
not assigned in astronomy; an unassigned arithmetic.

What kind of hollow library have you left me?
What kind of vacant texts are left?
How can I trust my own dear diaries? How
can I credit it or invest in each impression each
amended edition edit edit each repunctuated
unpaginated blank blank page? *Rescriptus*:
scratched and scraped again again. *Sa sa sa.*

Such nerve, such under new hand practice
to smooth reuse the washed and waxy pages,
wiping out and out my trivial fond recordings.
Here are my codices with biscuit crumbs
in the gathers, specks of hot milk, flecks of bran
engrained among the folded leaf of all of
all my recommended recommended readings.

You've erased – with repress and press – my tables;
retabulated all my bookish saws, all forms, all pressures
of proofs past and, by the uproots, pulled out
my base book. My sheer volume
is set back down, fainting from the worn paths
that eager youth and observation copied there.
And this is, this was, too true of all those from the ships.

Now bare memory bare recalls the feigned tract
of preformer and/or inferior original scripts.
I cannot trace me in my mark, and find my trailing
foot step dragged drawn and trained off crawling
course. You've remedied my mark,
made yours: *of those of those of those. Sa sa.*
Whose are these stranger fictions? And, who he?

Slowly though, slowly I recall and recollect:
a library without lenders – unrisked, inviolate –
a book unread – reserved from passage,
out of communication, incommunicado – would
enter lockdown, hot-boxed, cool solitary heel in hole.
So the Pelican Bay plexiglass on my supermax shelving
should dissolve itself into a dew, resolved by you.

So, go on, please handle all items with loving care
(both old and new). Touch and handle collection items
as much as possible. Only carry what you can't easily
hold. Stack up books, one on another. Place them
up side down. Use special weight to hold
hold pages. Please note: collection items should never
never be returned. And copying? copying is so so charged.

So catch up in the drift bite down the bait and hook
to tell the interfering bitter fish go fuck his feedback
loops loops deny his affective influence *rat-a-tat*
don't long long to redeliver perfume lost *rat-a-rat.*
Always a borrower always a lender be. Soft you now:
these were rich gifts rich pickings. So steal away.
Keep sucking bright honey from the vow. Steal away

all those from my ships.

VII. My grandfather's axe

All change. Up from my cabin, my sea-gown scarv'd about,
blue denim all unbraced, shirt pale of face, wearing
worn-out odd socks (quite like old John Locke, or not),
I grope and tumble in the dark for purposed purchase
dazed from noting your sudden and most strange returns.
Should I do it welcome? Thank you. Say, 'this was well done'?
Or, 'this was hostile'? Shouting, 'no, you've not done well'?

Everything has remained the same. Step in. Come in.
And not remained the same. Step in again. All change.
And as I thread up through the labyrinthine
boat up bark up bottom bowels, I start to dream
(I am a shattered fool I am to tell you this:
come in) that this ship is not my ship: that it too
has altered states – all change – bit and bit beyond belief.

Running a finger – the pink type face of which
is no longer the tip that touched your smooth skin
clear along the clavicle clean along the spine
that sloughed off and edged along your lip that dipped
among follicles on cuticle in cortex to medulla deepening
in hyaline Henle Huxley come in come in close-contact
in capillary in tense convex craving curve come in –

stroking a hand come in come in – the palm of which
is not the palm that kissed the smooth skin
clear – and running fresh eyes along the hull, the keel,
the hog, along the deadwood apron, along the planks
the canted ribs – come in – the sheered strakes, I am amazed
to find that what was clinker-built, landings lapped-on-lap,
that what was lapstrook riven timber – ash, oak, and elm – has

been replaced, renewed from stem to stern. You must have drawn
your draw-knives, your darkly augered drill bits fit, applied
the perfumed steam and vapour of low warm breath, and
with attentive fingers joggled out each plank by plank, calmed
from moorings, slow moving, stirring every gripe and framing, gently
thwarting each and every stringer out, a disturb to each flush feather-edge
from inspiring fingers; you replace shipskin in carvel smooth irresistance.

All change. Even low on bulbous bow, changed through foam –
pushed through charged sea which suffers a scatter
to come again come together, approaching to recede –
some violent hieroglyphist has written over *Theseus*
with scrawl of *Stella: or, The Self: or, Same.* They
removed the ram; even the figurehead has suffered:
an ibis becomes a bug-eyed boar. All change.

Now all this metamorphosed ship – altered quite –
carries evidence of your palpable entry, dear depart.
You've left long apparent hair on each and every pillow.
An echo impressed, embedded, traced through and through
the togs, the unresistant thermals. 'Deep affect'
on my emotive British Standard Scale. Koch postulates
'infectious' as my steady state, and hoists his yellow jack.

Even the knives in the cabin's cutlery drawer aren't mine,
are they? The axe in the grate isn't either. Is it?
The lantern looks new, more gibbous, somehow:
and this dog is not my dog! I gave you honest Crab;
you gave back Trey, Blanch, Sweetheart,
with their black and white bad mouthings,
their trundle-tails, their poisoned pens.

Whose boat is this? (There are over three million
shipwrecks on your – *on our on our* – oceans' floor.)
Is this my ship? (The guilty imprudent *Erika*
tendered thirty-one thousand tons of loving gilt out

along the innocent coast of France.) And does it matter?
(I may be longing lovesunk, scuppered, but your jewfish,
eels electric, your pelagic fish swim down around ocean alley:

down ocean freeze, among accreted abiotic adoration,
among devotion deposits in doting carbonate mounds,
ardent around the sunken skeletal 3D frame,
among synoptic fond relief, adoringly uncomposed,
around among built-up affectionate sediment, among
hot-caring coralline, sharp-adoring calcareous algae,
this cyanobacterium of kindness, of compassion, algaeous care).

Whose boat is this? It is not mine to mind it. Do come in!
Nor mine to mind or mend. I don't resent it. Not a bit by bit.
No need for 'All Stop,' Doria: this boat you've left me,
Molly, is the greatest, latest, fastest! Change all.
I know I claimed that here at 0320 GMT that here
at latitude 40 north 69 I needed IMMEDIATE ASSISTANCE
but, I've learnt to like the changes.

Glad I am not myself: I did adore a twinkling star
but now run mad, effaced in moonlight. Ring them.
I am not what I was. From now on now
no words, no words to wield my matter. Ring them.
Jack insists at my heartfelt sleeves. Jack gently laughs
– entombed far off there in the library's catacombs –
at *individual*'s entry in my brilliantly defaced encyclopaedia.

When I drew down the gangplank, when I issued
a lender's pass, I unsealed the envelope, allowed
influence and admitted extension, opened the skin,
the nervous nutshell, and exposed its kernel sap and seed –
from phellum to phellogen to phelloderm to cortex,
through periderm stem, through vascular cambium into xylem –
I welcomed the one serious kiss.

These are love letters: these are thank-you notes. Come in.
Wanted posters. These are *in memorium*, black-velvet tipped
– Alice, O profusion, all changed, we miss you everywhere –
and edged with storks. These are thank-you notes. Come in.
These are money orders, invoices admitting all and all indebts.
These are menus, thank-yous, mandates, madrigals for our many
many voices. Adverts. Accounts of – not loss or cost – but what you left

with those from the ships.

[Mnemon brought his books to Alexandria having inserted cryptic characters in them, in identical ink and handwriting.] Ptolemaeus the king of Egypt was so eager to collect books, that he ordered the books of everyone who sailed there to be brought to the original copy in the library with the inscription 'a [book] from the ships.' They say that a copy of the third book of the Epidemics has been found with the inscription, 'a [book] from the ships, as emended by Mnemon of Sidē.'

GALEN

VIII. As emended

[SCENE ONE: MY SHIP]

Late last night I lay on deck, hearing quick sea and static
so overborne yet still so slow so lit by terrific utterance:
perhaps we could have all of this and should be glad enough.
And it was raining (and would be, all night and morning until
all afternoon). And all the while the cadent fall – by chance
and circumstance – kept falling. Last night, at dogwatch,
caught up among the happenstance, amongst of all the very this.

All bright and tender stair-rods, and a black cloud stuffed
quick with darkness, rolling murmurs through curtainwall.
Late night, at hackwatch, I fell on deck, listening out at you:
you sea you static. Advisory-force 6 whistling along phone wires.
Background listening for posted ghosts. Asking:
are you impelled far off in stillness? do you catch cold
across our trunk-call? do you shudder as I swallow aspirin?

Last night awake on weather-deck in feedback spray and curr,
in wash of indistinct and cute responsive frequencies,
I was at storm-force, where TV antennae curtail back and break;
I was at hurricane-force, my roof peeled off; *in extremis*
clean debarked, clean lifted from the tarmac. But still
I still caught drifts of old still echoes, echoes on our line:
you still haunt out, still trace enigmas in the seabirds' call.

When on the sudden gape and flash a bawling noise of
bawling thunder (*clouds flap and tear and scrape their sides*),
spun lightning flushed full-long along my cracked sea-spine, and
tips the mast in coruscate diagonal. Extremely bright and all
extremely sheer and scintillate. Why does she strike the sea?
Ariel is up in the crow's nest, grinning his fiery embered eyes;
he thinks he knows, winks at it, and makes it so: *carajo!*

What a hit it was! pure accident, electrostatic incident.
Coragio! Just before, tense in the swelling present –
that sodden split meniscus moment where Ophelia floats
pre-*gnasci* among the phases of each capillary cat's-paw wave
all adhered still to the heavy concave crescent; or in the stuck
pause just before his sword declines, where Pyrrhus stood
neutral (as rack stands in stasis, bold winds and orb at hush)

– just before, I sensed the deck tense and atoms accumulate;
I heard, among the clouds, the ice and graupel rub and wail; I felt
our charged regions aggregate and equalise, cloud down to ground
(our electric potential must have been astounding to counteract such
high-resistance in the medium), then steep white runaways break
down and in hot-stepped jumped return strike out such wonderful
upward streaming. Ions pool around our leading fingertips.

Hot ions pool around damp lead tip. You hit: Cloud-to-Ground.
And off, off route and so we go, careered off track, quite kiltered
off to turn and back to turn about again, a thrilling rout:
Red box: I'm palpably thunder-strook. Yellow box: I'm palpably
struck by lightning. Blue box: one hit let loose the pigeons,
released the ravens, and scorched my white doves. Green box:
one hit on the stern-runway ramp and chryslers roll off into the wake.

So, holed below the loadline, punctured beneath the plimsoll,
I'm taking on water, foundering in the foam and break-up.
So, in dispersed in deep transverse across the shipping lane,
flotsam sloughs its curled path out: lost oarlocks loose in the drift; ballast
– gifts, notes, tokens, words, looks, and books of course, our books –
in long jettison loops; and strewn in the creeping shade of my hulling bark,
wineglasses instable sing among the ripples. Loving lines of jetsam.

Into the sea: eight culverins; two sakers; six fowlers; falcons, slings.
Iron murderers, hailshot pieces, and serpentines:
defences down, they all sink gently into bed. These will be pearls.
Fiddles and drums roll out behind the scuppered ship;
my broken ship upon my broken ocean. Pearls that were my eyes.
A trail of callipers, twin compasses, sounding leads, copied books,
describe my wayward swerved perverse parabola. Homeless

and unbound. The rain drops pass away (perhaps one day,
by labyrinthine chance, all this my sundry brightworked debris –
transoms, ribs, yards, prow, masts and oars all swimming –
will recombine among the alien crowd, brought back
together on sundering tidal matters: but till then, just drift). And
raindrops cool in ion pools upon my brilliant-cut, my tilted deck.
Shukran. What a hit. What amazing veer. What a way we had.

[SCENE TWO: YOUR LIBRARY]

So, strictly *entre-nous*, darling, how are you? You're hap back
among the bookcases, admiring your newly archived acquisitions.
You're back, admiring your text collections, conscripted docked deposits.
Along the cobwebbed aisles – clutching reading lists, shopping bags, swag bags –
squinting queerly at the titles and editions of all your fresh additions,
stacked under hot house arrest; making discrete enquiries
about what really matters; cataloguing all those from my ships.

And about you, your kleptomaniac bibliophiles restock an original library.
Among the spiral orbs of shelving, these slick bookmen weave and wander,
interleaving my lost texts into your fond recollections. And yes, I left, and find myself
a long way off in spindrift, away on aquamelt – fed out, spindled from heartstaff,
aimless on my dopamine dragline, spun out on spooling silken serotonin, ballooned
on vibrant tensile estrogen, on foxed oxytoxic protein traplines clued-out from you –
but trace the complex thread back – over an Aegean, across the Hellespont

through the wall's chink, and under the closed door – from gadfly me
to you. So here and now and now and then you realise: my rolled-out
sea-card plot, my led-out mazy pleat and plait, pricks our beat on a signal-line
shivered with limbic resonance, and, twin symphonic, snags tangles
in your intratext, intertwists its sticky coils, involves its looming toils
in all your tales and intricate narratives. You can't unpick it, though I wander:
this is the mortared *stoffe* – the pulp and dust – that both our dreams are made on.

Humming, hawing, buzzed by hurry, hunters stack and shelve my *camouflets*.
In his recess, one monkey-faced humpback incorporates my trashline drift,
conveyed in verbal camouflage, slipped among dead grey matter.
One archivist, indulging his hobbyhorse, scrawls *'elle a chaud au cul'*
in my Italian anatomy treatise; another effaces all named authors.
Even Doctor Dee is down there in the dark – quite sure he's not alone –
navigating, needing, reading pure verity at Sloane MS. 8, at Bodley 908.

But can these idiot aristarchs be trusted? Callimachus,
that cruel dissector, rips into things, crying 'big book! big evil!'
tearing strips, excising all my tortured scrolls; while, in blind rage,
Apollonius bites back at him, hissing: 'you discard, you plaything, you
mahogany maypole, cat, burr, you.' Demetrius defaces his own *History*,
deifying himself with a pen-stroke; while breathy Aristophanes plots,
drops random punctuation points in dashed *media disinctio* dots.

These masters of the books, these keepers of the tablets,
do they even spot the value of these texts? They check them in and out,
they surely stack them up and up, but can they even read these writings?
They seem so blithely unaware of what they've got – whatnots – and
barely note the subtle signs of Mnemnon's sleight hand, its crafty work,
dextrous in my margins, my ambivalent double-loded cryptic codes
of epidemic annotation emblazed amongst your careful holdings.

Remember me? *Ex libris* outcast, I'm all at sea, but in among your hoardings.
I may be cast off, laid off, ravelled out, dear departed headsail set,
spun out, but I'm all about between your lines, traced in your texts.
Castaway, I'm snared among woven planks of fir, mingled in the yarn,
twisted, threaded, and – smiling – sat so strange along the piece and pile.
Vagabond, I'm hard-wired in the circuit board; I'm right there in the tables,
a guest at the feast, haunting your studious spaces: remember me?

You're bound to. See, you've smuggled hectic honeyed hand-grenades
in amongst your alphabets, slipped bittersweet pharmaceuticals
into your own brilliant water supplies, and knocked back my gifts.
A stifled cry is heard down strangling aisles. Disguised as a librarian,
Sinon shows small-print coded contracts to my Mobman, to ProRat,
to Zeus and Koobface: my drive-by army armed and at your backdoor.
Remember me. You gently gently stole from me; and I steal back.

So check your holdings. I'm in ENGLISH LANGUAGE, blowing you a kiss.
I'm there in CLASSICS, giving you the eye. I'm up among RESERVED MATERIAL,
tipping you the wink. So check your spoil, your holdings 'cause I'm already in,
in behind the glass and lock and key of privy places, PRIVATE CASES.
I'm in LITERATURE, loving you. I'm in MATHEMATICS, loving you.
I set my life upon this cast. Threw all in, each sloughed eidolon and diced ion;
every sub-atom that spools among, pools among, cools among your catalogue.

So what a complex complicated haunting: my rebuilt boat;
your restocked library: our remade bodies; our emended lives.
I would like to write to you, so simply. And one day, bodies.
B1-C3. I we, on our knees; '*je nous écrit*,' you promised.
G1-F3. You we, lost at sea: 'you send me back,' I promised.
And to the fate B8 of love? Its seedy seasick *oooo*s and *aaa*s?
As to this, the simple fate of love: 'I'll write to you,' you promised,

'of all those from the ships.'

Puncture

We view the rock-paved highways worn by many feet.
We see how wearing-down
has minished them.

She picked out puncture
in the curve of worn stone steps,
that snagged the scene

and caught her with an attented hook and tug:
a soothed snag.
It took red dust, lucid air,

red air, parched grass, and lifted
all of them, to pinch their tuck, to nick
from guidebook and touch-up the map.

A snap, an instant capture.
A really represented. A naturalish truth
beyond the studious. Piercing glass.

Taut, the swerve and concave bevel
gave her stumble, brought her up short,
said 'what is' and then 'what was' and 'what has ceased to be.'

A tension from inclined tread under foot fall
lent something more than scenic
to *toppled masonry and ponderous stone.*

A cut, not cut but smoothed away
by punctual coincidence of foot and stone,
by accident of contact over time,

and fall of feet and feet and level rain
which flows and flows in mighty bend reverberate.
A shelled-out bruise, a bay,

a thumbed-out dip that gives each step
its line, its mine,
its distinct decline.

And caught, now, among these declinations, punctuations –
the spatial grammar of lateral column, horizontal wall –
she is what happens, what befalls.

And so, the hedging air is fetched
to forum
just to gaze on her.

And I know she pushed the groove
in with her heel, and felt it out
and lent it weight

(although I wasn't with her
and others were).
Just light hair, light shade, and cool concaved stone.

My mind is not deceived how dark it is, but
                              large hope
hath strook through my heart.

And I sat dumb stunned in a market place
and felt the vertigo of the earthbound
among the atoms' fall.

For lightnings pass through iron white-dazzles
rocks burn with exhalations fierce burst asunder
tottering in heat

'It is,' she said, 'what you wouldn't notice
unless you didn't look
that cuts across this drift and tumble.'

And I wish I was with you
when you glanced
and glance it.

And my hedging thought is fetched
to forum
to chance on you.

The pigeon with the peas

I.

It all falls quiet tonight
down in the sixteenth; and, up
on Trocadéro, *en plein air*, nothing new.

Just one burst dove beat
on-the-sudden rising:
a full squab clap, all wing-squall

of flustered fat *pipio* percussion
struck out in stocked air, as I pass. So, listen
as the bumblefoot beats and trips tip

to detonate quick on every upstroke,
to take soft pop and pump-up,
in oh-so coolest petrichor.

II.

But, look. Towards the Musée d'Art Moderne,
my radiant blackbody smoothes
through your Doppler surf, out

among your smartwaves of ultrasonic, out
along your nodal net and web mesh,
slipped out fast through the heterodyne hum.

I took to your turf to rap and bump
your cast-heart lockers, to
shimmy up and shiver up your glass.

Here, I dawdle past each tapped-up
winking watchman, evading each
their every unplugged lectric amber eye;

and they hear nothing, even as I
tease and tumble out
pins from the semantic stretchers, as I

strip out the semiotic shadowboxing,
jemmy the *passe-partout*; they're stone,
stone deaf to the soda lime crack, as I

peal away each prised picture,
snapped-so from the snug rabbet,
slipped from the happy frame.

Such soft and plastic larceny
undone down in the rosy dark,
drawn down elastic under covers:

my fingers are so full with
thick gesso nips and twists,
all oily in their rolling; my fingers

are so full,
        full of pigment, slick
with safflower, with heavy tug of pine;

        my hands
            are stained,
        full of wild beast,

        of tonal ultramarine
    and vermillion orgies, hit
        hit far beyond the blue,

                                  but you
                        don't even see
                                these trees?

III.

There's still no sign, no trace
of my absent old accomplice
idling on the avenue; there's

                no sound
of quick motors, running,
all gunned for our getaway;

                no auto-bandit ally
out in a warm night
along an empty esplanade.

'These five paintings are unsellable, sir.
You thief, you are an imbecile,
so now return them.'

IV.

Off-cuff, when I heard
the sound of peelers' heels
come crashing in my stairwell;

and heard all those bloody
bays and bloody rattles,
all flares of blues and twos

all wail and yelp and crackles;
and heard and heard
the short smart shock

of friction locks, and hammer's
cock, so sharp struck
by blackjack and Monadnock

so slap-jacked, slungshot
on the buckling buckling
backdoor, bootstrapped and

snap cracked, cracked
by kinetic *breach! breach!* as up
and up they came, all reeling hot,

all reeking pentrite, out
from their smoky mouse-holes,
and streaming streaming out

from their dusty doorways
to trail their reels of cordtex
all along and all along my heartstrings,

to drag detcord umbilical,
clean across and clean across
my heartstrings;

and when I saw – *blur blur*
between my bromide tears –
the surface play of surefire,

the kind trace of searching
streamlight cut wild through
my whirling smokescreens;

and saw each red hot dot slice
and slip the white phosphorus
in o dazzling o yellow tips;

and saw them [DUMMY TEXT] slide
across my [DUMMY TEXT] stoops
and trace my [DUMMY TEXT] missteps;

and when I saw and heard
the manganese prick and dance
across my ceiling, o'er my bed,

the sound of random-shock rippling
long around their digital airwaves
picking up on my long my long-gone echoes;

and when I blink blinked back
the channelled capsicum burn
of loss and vegetable love and loss

and blinked back along each
long peppered ion spool,
each keen-laced skein of mace;

              I ducked and
fixed my childish grin. I weaved, and
set my text. *I'll see you now*, I said, *come in.*

V.

And in they came,
the busy busy interpols:
Pinkerton and his Art Crime Team,

his book-club, reading-group,
FBI and IFAR squads incoming.
Monsters, sniffing up my staircase.

But, off-the-cuff,
I sold some dummy up
and deftly sloughed *Le pigeon aux petit pois*

        trash-down
        trash-down
        right to the compact.

The five pea cluster
that tucked up safe
among the shattering plate,

the claw that clawed at air
and beady peepings,
picked out in candlelight,

go gulping-down
some laundry hatch:
a lovely thing

      spat out
among the garbage,
the hawks of dear-darling rejectamenta.

Just as I told that bold brigade,
      those bandit catchers,
'I just panicked.'

And – cold, cold, my girl –
quick ditched
around four hundred million

pearls, pearls worth all my yeggman tribe,
dancing down the shute; green pearls,
blown in the silk.

VI.

This is appalling. Pastorals fall as
fans flicker, as olives tumble, and chandeliers
crush to crumble. But you said nothing.

And so I dumb-stood, fingers crossed
and bent back dumb double, tips crammed
in my stitched-up pocket's rubble,

all innocent with my blank-face,
my open open-hand – no jokers here,
no aces, no jacks, no tricks, no bluff –

just caught white-knuckled
in my Alcatraz coup, one short
of the full blitz, and not quite chunky,

just dropped, dumped down
and cold now – utterly unread –
in the coffeehouse. Turbid in the dregs.

VII.

There are no Big Winners! here, it seems:
we stale in the endgame stalled;
we leave, unachieved, and mere elliptical.

Perhaps it was those silent silent phone calls,
spooked me; made me chuck all in, and ruff it,
quite psyched by such high-stake publicity.

Resounds in the cross-wires, retorts on
the currents, caught in a cross-hair trigger:
I couldn't catch a risk, and folded.

These were unpassable paintings, you thief,
and I, sir, am an imbecile, quite
complexed at all my all extremes.

Unless perhaps the pigeon sits
somewhere or place, tipped off the market,
such hot-property, and ripe for a reset;

unless of course, of course,
she got away with wetwork, sits
smug with her grizzled mockers,

and turns her blue cheek – my *cher ami*
– slowly, to pay out one long last cupid line
towards her last her last hurrah:

unless, perhaps, the pigeon sits,
nap on her cedar stool, snug to the fence,
and screaming.

Still all still
down in the sixteenth;
and up

on Trocadéro,
en plein air:
nothing new.

Yellow Milkmaid Syndrome

During a survey the Rijksmuseum discovered that there were over 10,000 copies of [Vermeer's 'The Milkmaid'] on the internet - mostly poor, yellowish reproductions. ... This was the trigger for us to put high-resolution images of the original work with open metadata on the web ourselves. Opening up our data is our best defence against the 'yellow Milkmaid.'

Verwayen et al, *Europeana Whitepaper*, No. 2

There she is, intent, in all the right ways,
in her yellows, blues, and browns.
The milk she pours is true, runs white-to-creamy

—bright from your morning window, runs steady

in light the liquid flows

These days, she's coming quite the all-familiar
to homing sight,
proving ever ever-present, all correct, and quite

quite full, in-all,
and lost

in her every every cool, her concentrated colours

I.

Now, look up here – up here – and how, so soon, your soapy
search-search histories will trick, will trick 'n' hook, and ring.

See how, in finely filed and quite distinct derivatives, she comes
along, quick to the digital, freefloats from th' engine-room rollers

still filmy slick from such thin transit – her luminance, her liquid –
and, wrung-out, ranked on scroll, she run-runs the resale shelving.

Like this – tweaked on the tubes – like this – she seems to beam and
beam along your O-so-lovely low E-deltas, O cool in the cathodes.

But yes, she looks so different now – and different now – from
how she was, or even how she is, or as she deftly claims to be.

And all the top, these so-so hotly high-tipped hits betray, that
she's – truth to tell – no longer quite the fixed, the constant type,

and that – hand to heart – she must confess some sleight or slop,
some dot-pitch slip; to pigment clip;

                                    admit some tonal shift;

                                                            to

pinked tints in her pigment hues; to infinite shocks of diode drift
            in burst in brilliant blue;   to vivid variation:

                            to

                        soft shuffles in Triple-O, irresolute.

II.

People simply didn't
believe
that   the postcards
in   our shop
were showing
the   original.

Metadata should be seen
as advertisement
for content. As opportune.

And although potential loss
of phantom income
should be seen
as very real,

we don't
necessarily
want to make money
ourselves, but

for fear of loss

for very real

for real –
the very sake of us –

we do need
some on-tick faith-potential,
be it
in the post or simply touched to plastic

– so send   *so send me back, invested, and*   *send me back invested –*

for fear of loss
among the
this, this all
of metadata

The Best Defence against desire-jaundice
cultured in our scripting is
better data, till we credit it,
and open out
around   the original wound.

III.

Don't these, the very best returned results, just seem
so keenly smart in their high-fat saturates?   So
honest and so ever-so: safe as crystal-clean keepsakes.

How they ply impressive claims as no-fade photographics:
how they play and play, and lay and lie, and make
pretend as most ideal immaculates.

No mis-tones in the neat neat colour-coding here,
they say; all fixed, pinned in the pixel picked, and then
when wet to touch, as lawful as our art and apple-eating.

O yes   at 16:10   don't they then just rush so
red–red hot around a living-capture?   at 16:9,
an amber line adjusts towards a warm-ish orange blush,

out in the wash and dying, down to
an almost-burning umber loss: 4 to 3, burnt-out,   4 to 3,
by the very life of it.

You see the hex triplet shift, how bright hues lift lift
                         in the backlight, as the bytes down
           on her stiff-laced bodice bend, bow from the original orpiment

as the copy copy of her chroma-Form LightYellow turns and folds
                            LemonChiffon, turns
                            PapayaWhip, or Moccasin: finds

            Khaki

                            in the Gold.

IV.

'I am, I am *In loving memory of*; I am in place of;
                        in spite of;
           I'm in among the fond smears of thin-licked Vaseline;

               in glorious salty hyper-colour,
                 Epsom style;
               in thin-licked gelatine.

and yes, I'm digging down in the deep jammy aspic,
                 immemorial, preserving it all
                erroneously in its own odd terms.'

V.

'These days,' is it so important that you really *see* what stuff
her impassion is made of, to allow it how it matters?
Does it really tell to tell – from her first inventions,
           right through the dead-layers,

till we're strict to the touch-up –
the hard account of her?

After all, this girl, in apron strings, is hardly azurite; but
                                        is   amazing
ultramarine,   in rare quantities, crushed from *lapis lazuli*.
Might there then be something there, some thing or other
                    in the knowing-that,
                            in absolute acute appreciative accountancy?

I know some things: that something sculptural forms
                    among impasto
                        in the inclined invert of her face and forehead,
            which sits – impassive as any – beneath the weight
                                        of acid flake
        and warm mass-tone fold of lead-white linen: cerussite

skimmed from the reamy ferment coils,
        baked
                by tanner's bark, is
        lifted
    clear
from the boiled carbonics, clean to a spooling dazzle.

I know that shadow traces, grey-caked on the raw base layer are
            laced with charcoal,
            black-to-the-bone; that madder lips the greenish gray,
        built up from the dead colours in the cheap green earth
            unblended; that
            red sits by the whitened dab, tucked in to indigo.

I don't know if it matters much, or massively, to know
                    that carmine fades; that there is
                    arsenic in her yellows; an old worm in her red lead.
        Of course, the milk she poured was only ever
                        due to curdle, skimmed

from the absolute truth – but still

the brown bread – though thinly sliced – can
                                    cut up well across
        the wholegrain and synthetic substitutes, and bite
    and bite   just as memories hold
                                        on wonted place,
and often come
to fill it: with postcards of you,   tending to sheer yellow

VI.

And you, you just so close to the dead-cert deal, quite close in each
        and every lovely lovely detail, every detail
                                        but the real

With you, there was always a lookback trick,   to catch
at a glance-charge, to sneak at the lastgasp
                        voluble glimpses   – voluble –

to once more set in store   astonishing   snake-hair
                    in tumble-down stares.   I miss it. I miss it.

                        Yellow milkmaid syndrome.   I miss it.

The open door

                to that cool-stone kitchen – mass of arm and hip –
            should sure admit some sort of best defence,
        as my milkmaids gather,   gather in the guttering,

after all, we're ripping each fond loaf to starry pin-prick recollections
— *moldy tips pick white and scatter* —
splicing hot nostalgia into all our cakes and custards.

10,000 poems and postcards and poems and posts
from every shade, it seems, but you
— *corn-flowered up on each O every wall and stairwell of your bloody Rijksmuseum* —
10,000 in the last pitch alone alone,
and I've lost your bloody yellows

and it's not and not

enough, that I know the code she's
written in; enough, to know the make
of LEDs and leads that light you; enough,
the saturation of this colour, how it was
made, why it fades, its old name and its
new, enough enough the names of every
milkmaid as they fade

and yet, taut to the saturate,
lost to the steady steady,
she frames at one too many moves, at many more,

one step away inside the kitchen door, beyond the lintel,
and   so tight to her task, she stays
still   still

and is stayed, distinct in this instant's tincture,
each all entire to her own, intact among specific shades,
situated by a thousand shadows, of jug, breadboard, and mullion

brown jug, brown breadboard, brown mullion,
brown jug brown bread
each seed a point to loaded point   brown mullion   and cupids at her feet

Apart-of

I.

My left hand is always on the verge
of touching my right hand touching the things,
but I never reach co-incidence.

> How can you tell from;
> can you pick from;
> can you see for:

Between each interval
is a tree, and each and every and
act — O act — is gapped by scene by scene:

> so dancer, dance;
> chaff-up wheat;
> in trees, in wood.

Scene, the face around;
Scene, the vase around;
Scene, the line between.

> Apart of and a part from,
> we're beaten, you and I,
> like gold, beaten airy.

II.

We're lapped against each
in inspiration expiration,
sent out and posted back,

Count a car, then count
till car, and count
till car exhausts

and when I find you actual
under my hands, under my eyes,
up against and overlapped encroachment;

and are we counting cars, or
counts between cars? Between
each interval a car or tree or you and

when your eye and my eye envelop
such sparkled distances
and send such lovely letters then

me, driven from trunk to trunk
delivered to trunk by trunk
calls across embodied interims

we fold back recoil over,
and enter light and
am outside. And such
lovely grammar.

Vaucanson's duck

Monsieur Vaucanson, well-known for his automatic machines,
Has now come to this city to share with the Académie his plan.

Vaucanson's duck –   with wire-sprung neck,
with fragile hoops   declining;
unplumed, unflighted   by metalic fishbarb
of quill, of spine, *rachis;*   with panelled face
with plated eye   unsighted – sits still,
caught all up.   His brittle ankle
all caught up   in massive mechanism.

But soon, mesdames messieurs,   beneath
the lack of wings   each wheel on massy wheel
each steel cog tooth   – of face and pitch –
in bolted pig-iron ironframe,   will rachette up
and trip quick animation   in my automate,
sprung to lifelike.   With quack and flap,
its bill and beak,   its neb and tuck,
this plucked duck, with luck,   will up and up.

Motivation, emotion, move me.   Wind up
and up and into sinew   undulated strives.
Rhythmic lurches   unbind to wind out across
artful arch articulate.   Skeletal delicacy
moves, moved by   cranked energia.
And hefted to its shifts,   its punctual catches,
it pumps unfeathered wings,   pulled up
from webbed roots,   pneumatic plumps

chest puffed rebuffs   the big wind up and up.
And look, he's up away   pneumatic
with the breeze   that winds its currents
round coil electric   animate.

Catches, catches the drift.   so swerves.
Lucky strokes,   beat, stroke,
tucks swerve round accident   and off,
out of frame,   unbuckled.

Vaucanson   can't believe his duck,
and can't account its   indirections;
it flits our expectations, it   defies prediction
in wilful predilection   perverse inclination
inclined, clined,   declines decline
branch from root   misled, sent sideways,
lull, jolt, shoot out   in semantic skid and pull,
spelling out canards in   weasel-limbed whales.

He cuts across clouds   wetting his wings
on the rain drops they hold   and disrupting
a turbulent shower a cumulus.   His rupture
sends spray precipitous   cascades fall
as he writes his passage   diagonal
spinning in his scripted   wake.
Leaves Vaucanson   as a
startled   I.

In raking light

Change[s to a painting] may be so small that [they] can be detected only with the help of special lighting. One such means is so-called 'raking' light, a beam thrown across the surface and almost in the plane of it.

> George Leslie Stout, *Report of a Committee of Confidential Inquiry into the Cleaning and Care of Pictures in the National Gallery, 1948*

I.

I take the raked light
that cuts up black bright,
burnt beyond the violet:
a heat-seeker of

heart-change, of any second thought;
and as each freckled error
pops and comes to catch,
it picks up *pentimental*.

And, in the beam's fetch
the urgent silt sits up.
Its sketch lifts; it shifts;
makes surge-lines break, and drift.

The underdrawn in emergency.
Sure, there is plan enough down there.
Sure there is pain and error.
All gridlined, all locked in hotshock.

II.

Once, there was life here –
residual and errant –
hushed since, shucked under
the thick skin, the tough slough.

A past master lies licked in his dust.
Yoked behind slaked lime,
flake-white and linseed, hid behind
the chalking, quick lick-and-promise.

There was real life drawn here:
real big licks, happy hits,
blazing out carbonics, black
beneath what's now such dull dioxide:

me pinxit, a lonely migrant in-the-zinc.
Best lay on thick this body-colour,
wash up thick, inert, and bold to hold
back back the fugitive risings.

III.

But look as all these
red hot herrings
come rippling up
from the patio. Up

and out of their replete etymologies.
Such spot-lit crazy paving:
such soft loss and limescale,
lovelorn in our mossy grouting.

Look how it teases, tenting
in the fine acrylic fractures,
making milk-skin move
love from the facture.

With raking light, breaking.
It all comes out in the UV wash,
as kisses skimmed from
a stuffy undergrowth. Look.

IV.

Rushed up from a dead layer
pushed through grained teeth,
come breaking scrawls of
green *verdaccio* lettering;

ocra rosso spools, that pull from prime;
here come the loveliest pigments of
                    lightest *sinopia*
mixed and mulled, thin as water.

All this urgent urgent underwriting,
these gravid traces that track and slip
free from old amnesiac glazes, and slide
oblique along an oily oily traction.

Clear-as-day; evidently unrepentant.
Each word coughs up deep meanings;
verses crack in the dock; intentions
are admitted, and all clocks stop.

V.

So, go slick your radiant violet
lick through the lithopone, the
red-lead sediment of our repentance.
Love lies clear obscured by brittle films.

Look up, as all our raw composings –
tucked beneath the white wash,
the neat grins, the touch-ups
– come rising up to greet you.

Still I sense our all, our error,
drowned down in the underways
dabbed under the mass-tone stilled.
A whole whorl of love and life in fallow,

evaporating like wood-smoke
beyond the focus plain,
sunk behind the fat-and-lean,
yet not-lost down chrome yellow lanes.

VI.

At times, I feel the pink'n'pick,
an infrared of needleprick of
memory's ultraviolence. But, not now.
Not tonight, my neon Josephine.

At times, I speak, and look-outs shout,
as from each extensive word
a long lineal grass comes taut sprawling,
fired, out from fat obsolescence.

At oftentimes, some nothing moves.
No rustling mice in the columbines,
no sex in the tender scumbling.
The rake's ten tines come up gasping, 10x.

At othertimes, you frack up
fast in my undertone;
you find dirt tracks and
growl growl the dark corners.

VII.

So hot   is comes
    the bright hot hit
of raking light.
It beaming beaming.

It isn't all
of what I meant to write
      at all
            of beaming beaming.

This is, tonight,
the 'love-light' comes
in croons, sappy blooms, of slice
of ultrabright and beaming.

It ruffs, she roughs, and rakes and rucks,
        and right up beaming.
It isn't all of what I meant to write
        of all our brake lit dealings.

VIII.

My god, you must
                have heard
        how much I miss
the oxidizing glare, the hard tithonic:

                its strict emphasis
        that lit me
lit me right up, angular, choke cloak,
    in brilliant mercury-vapor.

You must still see
        all those bad bad intentions
                blazing: my blistering gilt
glows gold, picked up by black ray.

But tears restrained are worth
    as much as shed. And now,
        it is night out. And now,
        it is dead.

Pentimenti

~~I like the heat~~ ~~the tenderness~~ ~~the edible~~
    ~~the lusciousness~~   ~~[and bread~~
~~I like the wheatfields~~ ~~the plough~~ ~~the apricots~~   ~~—above all]~~
    ~~the shape of apricots~~
    ~~those flirts of the sun.~~

I.

So, trickster, there I ~~am~~ was
    tucked into the grass
        for you to glance at
      behind flat glass.

So, saboteur, there we ~~are~~ were
    sunk knee-deep in the inch-thick
        ~~fat to~~ ~~the gummy wooze~~
    made up full in the facture
        while each ~~daft~~
           eye draws to the door,
        while every eaves
           dropper snugs
              chop-chop to the rafters.

II.

Shush shush, the doggerel rush
      for one
        long
     swansong.

III.

We~~'re~~ were

at ~~one jump~~ one kick

beyond thei~~r~~ ordinary.

We ~~are~~ were

at jump, *right to* ~~*the ordinary*~~ *it*,

~~fingers~~ ~~loved~~ in the colour tone,

~~fists~~ ~~tight to the~~ high thrum,

~~limbs~~ lain twist in the warp,

~~all~~ in, at the first weave

stitched   and oh so starkly starkly

without a dry thread on.

IV.

I'm going further in   ~~Now, what then? Is this unclear enough~~

among black ~~orchids~~ violets,

among black hyacinths,

lurking in the opacity

of an overgrown orchard,

snapping

– with smart grammatic static –

into our interminable débris of revision

sinking

into the underdrawn.

V.

You – soft between the dials
        and tentive to the redials –   ~~– your number, caller, pl~~
slipped me soft off hook
switched clear off a clean step, and
left me lost out here;
       ~~– dialling, dialling –~~
left me   out of each
       and every key exchange, to loop
~~and loop~~ locally through each
        of every bad bad branchline's reach. ~~– what number, e~~
     So wrung out rung
  in starkstruck reroute
     right round such nerve-
     taut tough telephonics, O,
        such livewire centres,
      O, such rough rate centres,
       such awesome plugboard din.   ~~– num~~

    ~~O PBX, PBX, there surely may~~
      ~~and surely must~~
       ~~be some soft or slubbered sort~~
   ~~of authenticity, my darlin', darlin',~~
     ~~around about, 'round here, somewhere?~~

  ~~There surely must and may well be~~
    ~~some simple truths, beyond the~~
      ~~online etymologies, the~~
    ~~phoneme slip and slide:~~
~~where word derives, home from home,~~
    ~~rote rives, from home to home,~~
  ~~cuts down beside, to hide, at home~~
      ~~and home and home.~~

VI.

and so, this should be seen
                    as
                        all wild-eyed in capped
                                    careen
                        unhushed, and come
                    as
                        a fairly desperate dive,
                        a last gasped finely final call –
                                    falling galled appalled
                                            in dumb steamed crambo –
                    as
                        comeback come back
                        please:
~~   as~~
~~   one for the road.~~

VII.

~~But~~ This then stands around
                    like a late careering
                            hit against hope;
                        a shot sliced
                        askance to the fine grain;
                            adrift to the rainfall, just
                                a doe-struck call-back reeling
                            back to the clumsy couch,
                                    to hot drops on the plastic roof –
            with no puns intended there,
                    just flesh and hipped bone,
                        pushed along together –
                                            back to rude things,
                                            that mattered,
                                            raw things, lost.

VIII.

What, so I'm grown so tonedeaf in ringdown?   ~~your number ple~~
what, so I'm so lost in switch, so lost
            so lost to the patchcord crossfire   ~~number ple~~
that you slip the ringing cord,
        that you drop the rear cord
            slot to the hot electric jack –
                and there, among sharp static,
                    this buzzbell and fedback feedback fuzz,   ~~can you hea~~
                    that I'm calling?
            Out in the wire world.

IX.

Your lips, step out of cinch,
            broke clinch, but
        I still mouth around for
            our lovely
            wordstuff, unreturned.

X.

                        Dialled right on up
                        to ~~hot~~ cool-blue
                            booty.

                        Keeled right up right up
                        to your ~~hot~~ neon-tips,
                        your ~~hot~~ fluorescent
                        that peels off
                        among these
                        screeds

and ravelling
        ravelling
under their radars,

off their cold cut
   ~~tender~~tenterhooks
   ~~and maybe even key and colour,~~
      ~~and scale and chart,~~
         ~~hale and heart,~~

    the one last peaky tentation cast
    off in-coming kiss-me-quick
    raiders homing in, in

      stealthy
    for even such an even-chance
    of such a ~~hot~~ catch-up.

XI.

I've sent a photo. Of hungry me,
starved in dark flowerprint,

lapped, shoulder-to-shoulder,
    against this love-child, bastard boy,

all slick-backed boot-blacked bastard
whose fingers finger rosemary or

columbine, withered violets, held up
for ~~his fled father~~ an absent husband.[1]
Maybe the haunting eyes have it:
    remember me?[2]

125

Maybe the fine-thread fingers,
     the thinning veins?

I've sent some snapshots – hot
     'cross your beaten brows –

   to remind you
      of our garden.[3]

How every tree was hung
      with a mother's strong son,

   and all our furniture
decked-out with poisoned brothers:

     relics
strung out in the branches,

momento mori
     in the sun-strewn bows and beds.

To remind you of patios,[4]
      bedrooms.[5]

Oh oh oh lap spread, touched-off
        safflower in startlebright,

     all whiteflare under dumb paws,
and you can be Gorky's dead mother,

bland-eyed and bland-eyelid,
     and you won't stop sliding.

XII.

~~And you won't stop sliding.~~

Incrementally edged out,
 hedged off, your shoulder,
  – slow elbowed on hardline
   in thick coldpale – gets well drawn
   over and redrawn-over, well defaced,
    touched-up-well over decades.

     And your face-scratched
        buff to a polish.

     ~~And you won't stop sliding.~~
     And your pinked shift dazzles.

    And all your yellows scumble
  and look to lose touch.

        ~~And you slide.~~
  Deflowered, fibrous. ~~And you won't stop.~~

   In gradual shifts,
     lapsing out across a
  hook-tendoned interim that ~~dis— de-~~
  composes wider wider,
      and you won't
  stop sliding,
    with attenuated tolerance on
  tensive heartstrung sliding.
       And all your
  yellows out o out across the minded-gap
  that,
    with each amendment,
         only

increases, layer on layer by inchandinch,
until,
    by the time he died
        (hung up in Connecticut)
                thetwofigures –
childandmother – stand apa   rt
contact erased

                  their touch
paintedoverandover, as his mem   ory
of her
fades   and
            she won't she won't
            she won't
            stop
            sliding

Acknowledgements

Thanks are due to the editors of the following publications, where some of these poems first appeared. 'Glanced' and 'Tact': *PN Review* 216, March–April 2014. 'Of those from the ships', 'Glanced', 'Tact', '*Rete mirabile*', 'Puncture', and 'Vaucanson's Duck': *New Poetries VI* (Carcanet, 2015). '{{du | he |tao}}': *PN Review* 228, March–April 2016. '*Argus Panoptes*': *PN Review* 229, May–June 2016. 'Yellow Milkmaid Syndrome': *Blackbox Manifold* 17, winter 2017.